Doug Coates was born and educated in England and, after university graduation, worked as an architect in England and, subsequently, in Ethiopia and Singapore as a university academic, and in New Zealand and Australia in architectural practice. He has travelled widely and has also worked as an IT Manager and Business Continuity Manager.

Doug has bachelor's and master's degrees in architecture; and other pursuits include jazz guitar, sailing and woodworking. Doug is married, has two sons, and is now retired in Sydney. In Ethiopia, Doug collected many small silver neck crosses which are the subject of this book.

Copyright © **Doug Coates** 2025

The right of **Doug Coates** to be identified as author of this work has been asserted by the author in accordance with sections 77 and 78 of the Copyright, Designs and Patents Act 1988.

All rights reserved. No part of this publication may be reproduced, stored in a retrieval system, or transmitted in any form or by any means, electronic, mechanical, photocopying, recording, or otherwise, without the prior permission of the publishers.

Any person who commits any unauthorised act in relation to this publication may be liable to criminal prosecution and civil claims for damages.

A CIP catalogue record for this title is available from the British Library.

ISBN 9781035872152 (Paperback)
ISBN 9781035872169 (ePub e-book)

www.austinmacauley.com

First Published 2025
Austin Macauley Publishers Ltd®
1 Canada Square
Canary Wharf
London
E14 5AA

My thanks to Richard White whose collection, enthusiasm and help started my own interest in Ethiopian neck crosses all those years ago in Addis.

I acknowledge the contribution of those listed below in encouragement, information and images that have assisted me in the writing of this booklet:

The unknown numbers of Ethiopian artisans who have made *birr maskal* through many centuries.

Richard White whose collection and help started my interest in neck crosses.

Graham Romanes, former Honorary Consul-General, Australian Consulate, Embassy of the Federal Democratic Republic of Ethiopia.

Rod Waddington for inspirational photographs of Ethiopia.

The authors listed in the bibliography.

Contents

Introduction
- Motivation and Background — 8
- Map of Ethiopia & Eritrea — 11

Origin and History
- Adoption of the Coptic Religion — 12
- Categories of Ethiopian Crosses — 14
- Neck Crosses and the Metab — 16
- Maria Theresa Thalers — 17

Forms and Elements
- Basic Forms of Crosses — 19
- Morphology of Neck Crosses — 23
- Arm Variations — 24
- Crown Embellishments — 25
- Arm Terminals — 26
- Infills — 27

Methods, Styles and Localities
- Methods of Production — 28
- Styles and Localities — 33
- Common Styles — 34

Examples
- Crosses Illustrations — 37
- Small Crosses Illustrations — 66

Bibliography — 70
Weblinks — 73
Collections — 75

Introduction

I have used the spelling "Addis Abeba" in the following pages, although the name of the capital of Ethiopia is now commonly written as "Addis Ababa".

During my time in Ethiopia, students many times corrected me when I used the spelling, Addis Ababa.

The name, in Amharic, means "New Flower"
i.e., Addis = New;
and Abeba = Flower
whereas the word "Ababa" in Amharic means "Father".
In Amharic text:

አዲስ   አበባ
A ddi s   A be ba

Not:

አዲስ   አባባ
A ddi s   A ba ba

Motivation and Background

My intention in writing this book is to describe and catalogue Ethiopian neck crosses to the extent that I am able to, based on my own collection, on what knowledge I acquired in my years in Addis Abeba (within the limits of my memory) and on the limited information I have been able to find in books and obtain from sources on the internet. My interest is in the craftsmanship of the crosses rather than the religious significance (which is well-documented elsewhere). Unfortunately, my several attempts to contact individuals and institutions in Addis Abeba for additional information were unsuccessful.

This is not a definitive nor authoritative account but I could not find a similar discussion or record elsewhere; so this record might be of value as an outline description and compilation of examples of these works of craftsmanship.

I lived and worked in Addis Abeba from 1969 to 1973 in the Department of Architecture and Town Planning of Haile Selassie-1 University having first spent a short time there as part of a student expedition some years before.

An American friend in Addis Abeba, who had by then worked there for some time, already had a collection of silver neck crosses - *birr yangat maskaloch* - and took me to the Addis market - the Mercato - to show me where he, from time to time, bought them from one or two of the stall holders; and I started a small collection myself.

The neck crosses varied in price depending on size, pattern and condition (and the bargaining skill of the buyer) but were affordable and were an attractive item to collect and display; and it was possible to collect many different types through many visits and hours of bargaining in the Mercato.

After acquiring about 50 crosses, it became progressively less frequent that I could find different ones from those I already had, although I sometimes found replacements in better condition for some that I had previously bought.

The Coptic Christian females and many males of the Ethiopian highlands commonly wear small silver crosses on a chain or cord (a metab) around their necks. The metab is, itself, an item of religious significance. The crosses are of many patterns, some of which are said to be typical of particular localities, and are of various sizes from about one centimetre to about eight centimetres in height. The very small crosses are often worn by children.

While wearing of the crosses is a feature of the religion of the highland Coptic Ethiopians, the silver crosses can, if necessary, be traded in markets and are available for sale. There are also larger hand-held crosses, most often of brass but also of iron or carved wood, and large processional crosses of brass or silver which could sometimes be bought in the Addis Abeba Mercato.

There are gold mines in Ethiopia and there are many goldsmiths and silversmiths in Addis but the source of silver for making crosses was primarily Maria Theresa Thalers, and these coins could also be bought in the Mercato.

Faint signs of the original embossing on the Thaler could occasionally be seen in a silver neck-cross that had simply been cut from a coin but insufficiently polished, although more often the coins were melted and poured into clay moulds, making each cross unique even if of a local pattern or style.

The crosses varied from simple plain unpatterned ones to elaborate designs with 'endless-cord' filigree or inscribed patterning, crosses within circles and medallion-like patterns, to built-up hollow crosses with teardrop-shaped arms.

I have tried to find more information about the locality/origins of the various styles of silver neck-crosses but without much success. Museum collections in Addis Abeba (and elsewhere) are mostly not extensive and do not have much detailed descriptive information about the small silver crosses and generally do not identify the source locality of a cross other than the Axum and Lalibela styles.

In Ethiopia, neck crosses are so ubiquitous that, simply being so common a feature of Ethiopian life, it might seem difficult to catalogue and describe their variety. However, their many styles, origins, individual uniqueness and craftsmanship are such as to merit being recorded as an item of cultural importance and, hence, my attempt to do so.

Now, more than 40 years later, Ethiopian silver neck crosses are available for sale via the internet at substantially higher prices (although many are of low quality and apparently "manufactured" for internet sale).

Disappointingly, I have found comments that many silver crosses were being melted-down in Addis Abeba for their silver value due to increases in the price of silver. If that practice were widespread, it would result in a substantial cultural loss, with museum and private collections representing an important repository of these exceptional artefacts.

Doug Coates
Sydney, Australia
2024

Map of Ethiopia & Eritrea

The 13 Provinces and Eritrea and, in addition to the Capital, Addis Abeba, the provincial towns where known styles of crosses are reputed to have originated.

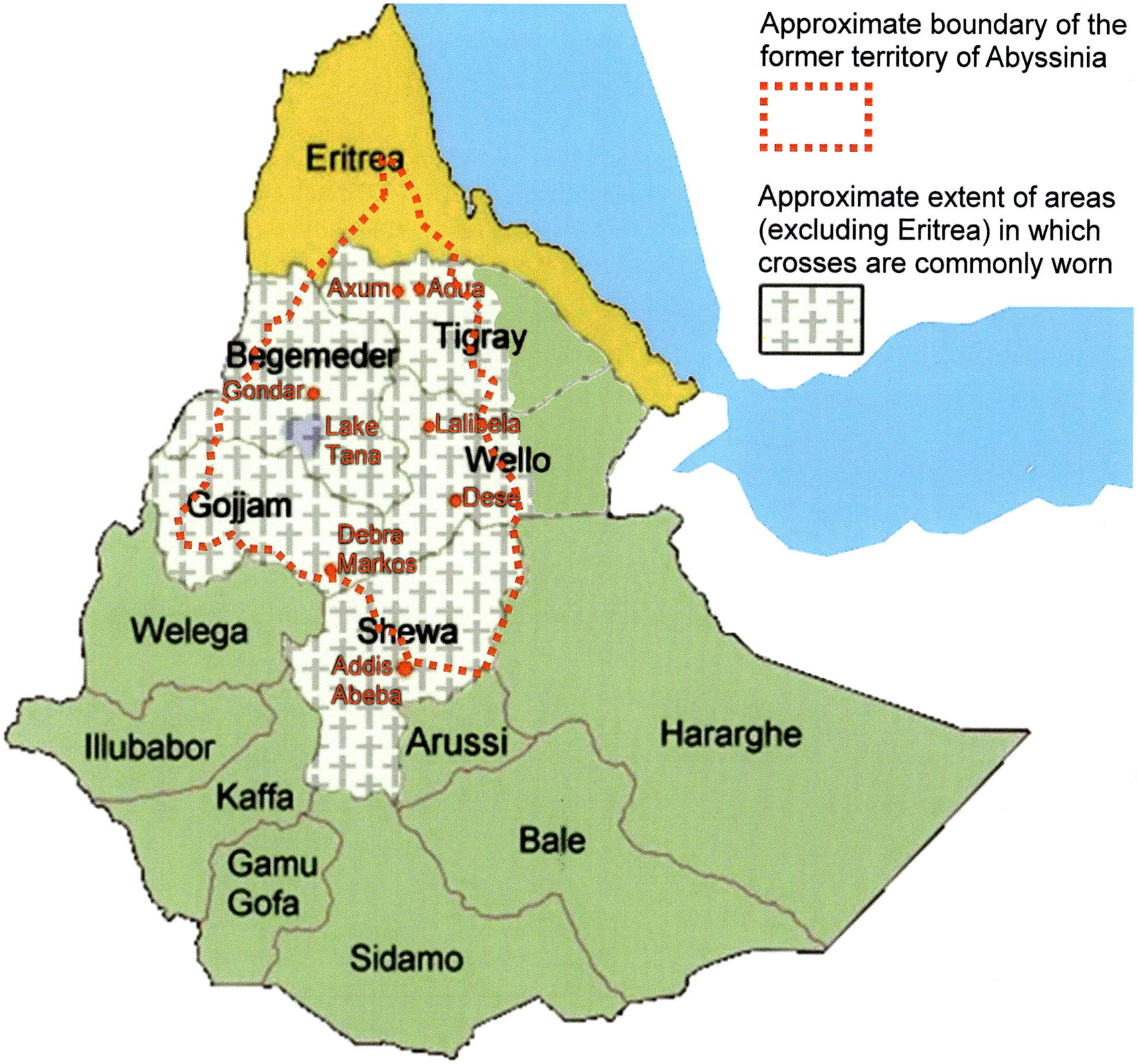

Eritrea, which was formerly the northern province of Ethiopia and its Red Sea coast, seceded from Ethiopia in 1993.

The extensive Kingdom of Aksum in the 4th century included northern Ethiopia, Eritrea, northern Somalia, Djibouti, Yemen, southern Saudi Arabia, northern Sudan, and southern Egypt.

Origin and History

Coins of the reign of King Ezana. Note the change from the crescent symbol on the coin above to the cross on the coin below following the adoption of Christianity.

Reproduced from: *commons.wikimedia.org/*

Adoption of the Coptic Religion

King Ezana of Axum ruled the Axumite Kingdom through the middle years of the fourth century AD. Ezana conquered Meroe - the capital of the Kingdom of Kush in present-day Sudan - and established the extensive Axumite Kingdom which included much of present-day Ethiopia, Eritrea, Djibouti, Yemen, southern Saudi Arabia, northern Somalia, northern Sudan and the southern part of Egypt.

Although Ezana is not named in the Ethiopian King Lists (e.g. List of Ethiopian Kings by H.I.H. Tafari Makonnen [later, Haile Selassie], 1922, in the publication *In the Country of the Blue Nile;* by C.F. Rey), coins minted in his reign bear his name which is considered synonymous with Abreha Atsbeha.

King Ezana was the first king of Axum to adopt Christianity and he appointed the Syrian Christian Frumentius as head of the Ethiopian Church. Ezana is regarded as a saint by the Ethiopian Orthodox Tewahedo ("Unified") Church.

With the adoption of Christianity came its symbol, the cross. Except in a brief period of Catholicism, it was almost never in the form of the crucifix, but was widely adopted in the Ethiopian highlands in many forms - as processional crosses, architectural adornment, devotional hand crosses carried by priests, neck crosses, tattoos, embroideries, paintings and carvings; and in several materials - wood, metals (gold, silver, bronze, brass and copper), stone, fabrics and painting.

In all these forms and materials, Ethiopian crosses evolved into a wide variety of shapes and patterns unequalled elsewhere, some distinctive of particular towns and localities, with incorporated symbolic elements such as various cross forms, circles, endless-cords and symbolisms of the 12 apostles.

While Ethiopia has several population groups and variations of culture, the Coptic religion of Ethiopians of the central highlands is an indelible aspect of life.

The Ethiopian year is marked by Coptic festivals, in particular Meskel, Timkat and Fasika, in which the processional crosses are very evident and paraded.

The Ethiopian New Year begins on Meskerem 1 on the Ethiopian calendar, which is 11 September in the Gregorian calendar. It marks the end of the rainy season and the beginning of the Ethiopian Spring but, two weeks into the month of Meskerem (on September 27), is the very important religious festival of Meskel (the Cross) which commemorates the finding of the crucifixion cross, an averred fragment of which is kept in the monastery of Gishen Mariam in the north of the country. Meskel and the festivals of Timkat (Epiphany) and Fasika (Easter) are substantial events celebrated by millions of Ethiopians.

Crosses, of various kinds and in various forms can be found and seen everywhere through the highlands, worn, carried, displayed in clothing and on buildings; and those worn as neck crosses by many Ethiopians are the most numerous and varied.

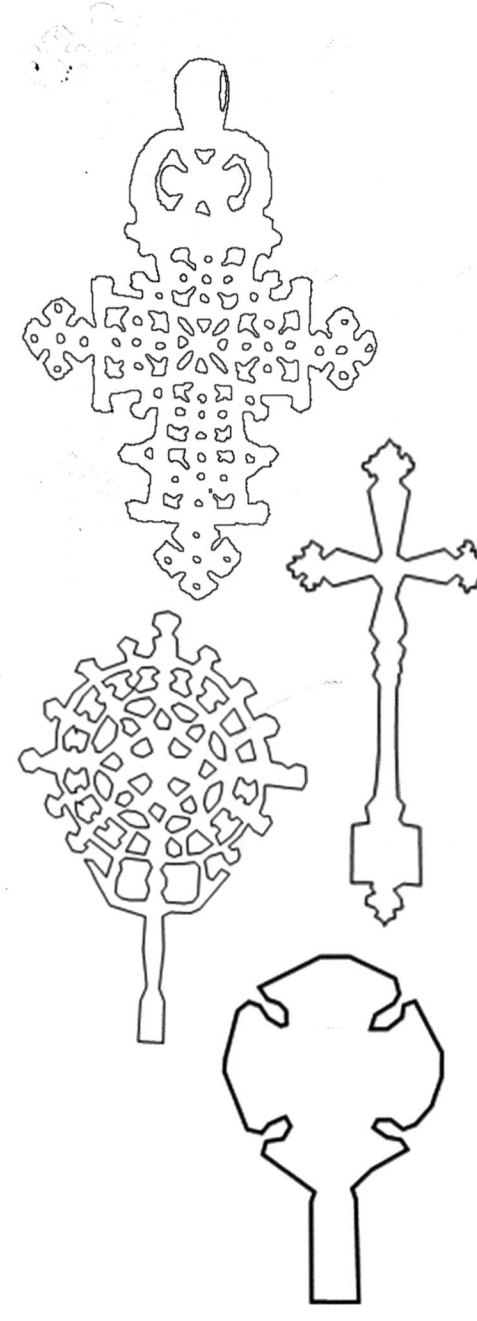

Categories of Ethiopian Crosses

Researchers and writers have categorised Ethiopian Crosses in several ways.

Buxton (1949):
Processional, Priest, Pectoral

Petrides (1960):
Pendant, Pectoral, Pastoral, Processional, Architectural

Moore (1971):
Processional, Hand, Neck

Korabiewicz (1973):
Manual-Processional, Manual, Processional, Pectoral, Apex or Architectural

Hecht (1990):
Processional, Hand, Pectoral, Apex, Architectural, Neck, Staff, Tattoo, Embroidered, Manuscript

(Similarly, Skrobucha and Heinz)

Overall, there tends to be some categorisation consensus regarding crosses as objects (i.e., excluding tattoos, embroideries, paintings and carvings) into four groups:

- Processional Crosses
- Hand (Priest, Manual) Crosses
- Neck (Pendant, Pectoral) Crosses
- Architectural (Apex) Crosses

Processional Crosses

Processional Crosses are the largest, most elaborate and impressive and, perhaps for that reason, they have been documented and illustrated in many publications. They typically consist of a metal cross on a wooden staff and are mostly of an intricate filigree design incorporating several symbolic elements described below such as various cruciforms, circles, endless-cords and representations of the 12 apostles. They are used by priests in ceremonial processions.

Hand Crosses

Hand Crosses are smaller, about 120mm to 200mm in height, and made of metal (iron, brass and sometimes silver) or sometimes of wood. Priests carry them in their daily work and often hold them out for Ethiopians to kiss.

Neck Crosses

Neck Crosses are the most abundant and exist in a wide variety of patterns. They are generally metal, most often silver. The cord, or metab, on which the cross is suspended around the neck, is an important symbolic element for Ethiopians and was itself a sufficient symbol of the wearer's Christianity.

Architectural Crosses

Church buildings in Ethiopia are sometimes of quite simple and modest construction, e.g., wood or mud plaster on timber, or timber frame and corrugated iron, and are invariably topped with a cross at the apex of the roof. Cross shapes are also used in windows and often in wooden panels in shutters, doors and screens and in door panels of icons and triptychs. Church buildings built of stone often have crosses carved in the stonework and crosses are painted in the interiors.

One of the most dramatic architectural instances of the cross is the plan form of the church of Bete Giyorgis (St George) among the Lalibela rock churches.

Ethiopian lady with a small silver cross on a blue metab and tattooed necklaces and tattooed cross on her forehead

Photo: Rod Waddington:
Orthodox Tattoos, Tigray, Ethiopia; 2015

Neck Crosses and the Metab

Neck crosses, worn on a cord around the neck, are the most numerous and best known of Ethiopian crosses. A blue cotton cord, "metab", tied around the neck of baptised Christians, has been the outward symbol of faith since early Christian times. A cross, or sometimes a metal bead, may be threaded onto or suspended from this cord.

In the 15th century, Emperor Zara Ya'qob (1434 – 1468) ordered that every Christian in the kingdom should wear a neck cross, thus identifying Christians from others. Copper, bronze and gold crosses of antiquity have been excavated in Ethiopia, but most likely a majority of the poor wore crosses made out of wood or had crosses tattooed on the body.

From about the same period or even earlier, the metab has had importance at least equal to neck crosses as a sign of the wearer's Christianity. The consensus among several travellers and observers from the mid-1800s onwards suggests that the colour of the metab was usually blue or dark blue and that silk was the preferred material. However, metabs were also often white; and cords made of three different-coloured strands, representing the Trinity, were also used.

Chojnacki *(Ethiopian Crosses: a Cultural History and Chronology)* provides much more information about metabs.

The Maria Theresa Thaler

In the 19th century, silver thalers ("dollars") of the Austrian Empress Maria Theresa became common currency in the countries of the Horn of Africa brought to those countries from Europe by various traders and expeditions. In Ethiopia, the large numbers of thalers became the primary source of silver and were melted down, often alloyed with other metals, or cut and filed to make crosses which were widely used. Even today they are still melted down by the many Ethiopian silversmiths to make modern silver pieces.

The Maria Theresa thaler - locally called *siet birr* (women silver) - is first recorded in circulation in Ethiopia from the reign of Emperor Iyasu II of Ethiopia (1730 - 1755). According to Traveller James Bruce, the coin was common in the areas he visited in 1768. Joseph Kalmer and Ludwig Hyun[1] estimated that over 50 million coins minted until 1931 ended up in Ethiopia. In 1868, Field Marshal Robert Napier's military expedition to Magdala, the capital of Emperor Tewodros II, took Maria Theresa thalers to pay local expenses. In 1890, the Italians introduced the Tallero Eritreo, styled after the Maria Theresa thaler, in their new colony Eritrea, also hoping to impose it on their commerce with Ethiopia but were largely unsuccessful. In the early 1900s, Emperor Menelik II unsuccessfully attempted to mint a Menelik version of thalers locally.

Maria Theresa thalers were 833.3 parts pure silver per 1000 (and a copper content of 166 parts per 1000). Sterling silver, the silver standard in England since the 15th century, has about 10% more pure silver at 925 parts per 1000. The thaler is about 40mm in diameter and 2.5mm thick, weight of about 28grams and contains 23.39 grams (0.752 troy ounces) of fine silver.

Maria Theresa Thaler at approx full size

[1] Hyun, Ludwig and Kalmer, Josef, *Abessinien, Afrikas Unruhe-Herd,* Verlag "Das Bergland-Buch", Berlin 1935

Maria Theresa reigned from 1740 to 1780. Thalers were first issued in the first year of her reign in 1740 and then re-issued until 1780.

Maria Theresa thalers continued to be issued after her death in 1780 but all are dated 1780 regardless of when or where they were struck. Maria Theresa thalers were issued in Vienna, Prague, Florence, Milan, Venice, Rome, London, Paris, Brussels and Bombay.

One suggested explanation of this unusual practice of the repeated standardised date of a coinage is that African populations, including Ethiopians, having agreed to accept the thaler in payment for goods and labour only after minute inspection of the coin, refused to subsequently accept a coin which was different in respect of the changed date.

Authorities estimate that 400 to 800 million thalers were issued between 1778 and 2002, when the Austrian mint issued 14,924 "new" coins.[2]

Silverman and Sobania in their Journal article *Mining a Mother Lode: Early European Travel Literature and the History of Precious Metalworking in Highland Ethiopia, page 346,* describe interesting details about Maria Theresa thalers and their use in silverwork in Ethiopia.[3]

Every cross illustrated in the examples in this collection is less than the weight of a Maria Theresa thaler.

[2] Ref: https://en.wikipedia.org/wiki/ Maria Theresa thaler
[3] *History in Africa,* Vol. 31 (2004), *Mining a Mother* Lode pp. 335-355, Cambridge University Press

Forms and Elements

Basic Forms of Crosses

There are many forms of crosses. Many are variants of basic forms such as those listed and illustrated below and these examples are also found in the four categories of Ethiopian crosses (Processional, Hand, Neck, Architectural).

Latin Cross
The three upper arms are of equal length but the lower arm has extended length.
All the arms are orthogonal and of consistent width.
This is the most common depiction of a Christian Cross in modern times.

Greek Cross
All four arms are of equal length.
All the arms are orthogonal and of consistent width.

Patée Cross
The equal length proportions of the four arms of a Greek Cross but with splayed arms.

Gammadion, Fylfot, Swastika
An ancient Hindustani symbol adopted by the Christians in the catacombs and ancient cemeteries because it contained a cross that was disguised from their denigrators and enemies.

This symbol has been used by many cultures over many centuries.

Coptic Cross

Old Coptic crosses often incorporate a superimposed circle; sometimes large, sometimes small, which is derived from the Egyptian Ankh, a symbol of life.

A second Coptic cross is widely used in the Ethiopian Coptic Church. It is composed of four arms meeting at a circle with Tau-like crosses in the quarters around it. Many Ethiopian Copts have the cross tattooed on the inside of their right arm.

Celtic, Ionian, Irish, Halo, St John's or St Columba's Cross

This is similar to a Latin cross with an imposed centre circle. St Columba, who died in 597 AD, founded many churches and monasteries in Ireland and Scotland, the most famous of which was on the island of Iona.

Budded, Apostles, Lazarus, Treflee, Trefoil or Bottony Cross

A form similar to a Latin cross with the addition of trefoils (derived from the clover-leaf and similar plant leaves) at the end of each arm.

Iota Chi Cross

The name is derived from the superimposition of the two letters iota (**I**) and chi (**X**), in the Greek alphabet—the initial letters for Jesus Christ: iota: **I**ησους (Jesus) and Chi: **X**ριστος (Christ).

Circle Cross, Cruciform Halo, Ringed Cross or Nimbus

Ethiopian crosses also include a circle form with an internal cross of which the arms may extend beyond the circle, similar to the upper portion of the old Coptic cross and to the upper portion of the Celtic cross.

Diamond Cross

Ethiopian crosses also include a diamond form with internal cross and sometimes with extensions outside the corners of the diamond. More elaborate diamond-shaped crosses are also common particularly in larger processional crosses.

Positive and Negative

Also known as *Solid-and-Void or Figure-and-Ground*. For each of the cross forms illustrated above, there is a positive form in which the cross is the "solid" and the spaces are formed by "voids" or some background material; and there is the negative form in which the cross is formed by the "voids" and the background between the arms of the cross is formed by solid material.

A particular and frequently used instance of this solid-and-void patterning is a form of the Patée cross in which the voids (the white triangular spaces in the example at the middle left) form the Patée cross between the diagonal "X" of the solid material.

There are also many instances of crosses (of the Greek equilateral type) set diagonally in designs in both positive and negative form and as engraved marks.

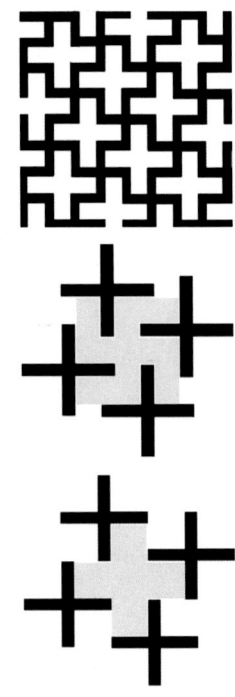

Arrays of crosses

Arrays of cross-shapes are sometimes used in patterns or in carvings or carved screens. When set out in arrays, secondary patterns are formed by the spaces between the primary shapes. Examples are:

Multiple linked Swastikas (black lines) form enclosed Greek crosses (white spaces).

Arrays of Greek crosses (black lines) imply enclosed Swastikas (grey spaces)

or imply enclosed Greek crosses (grey spaces).

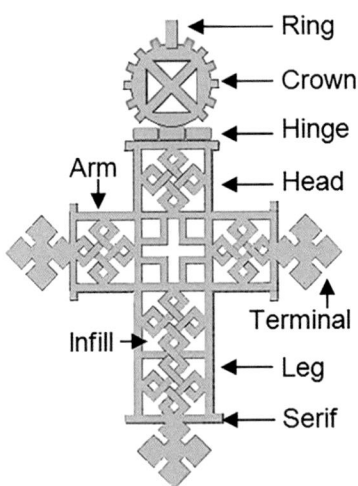
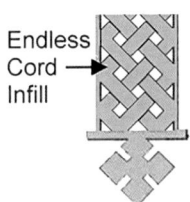
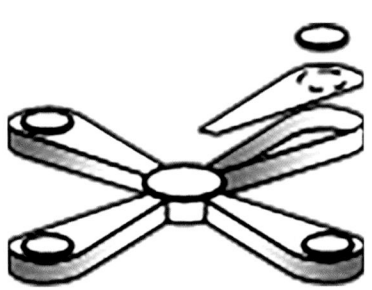

Morphology of Neck Crosses

Not all Ethiopian neck crosses have all the elements shown in the diagrammatic illustration, but the more elaborate crosses do. The naming of the parts is not formal but is for discussion purpose only. The illustration represents a formal cross shape but the body of some Ethiopian neck crosses may be diamond-shaped, or circular and medallion-like.

All neck crosses (unless damaged) have the ring, through which a suspending cord (metab) or a chain is threaded.

The crown may itself be of an elaborate design and incorporate a cross, an infill lattice or continuous-cord infill. It may also have small embellishments around the perimeter, sometimes symbolising the twelve Apostles or sometimes representing birds standing in profile.

Most neck crosses are made as a single solid object but some, especially larger crosses and the circular medallion style, may have a three-segment hinge between the crown and the head of the cross. Some crosses appear to have the crown silver-soldered directly onto the cross in a way that suggests there was originally a hinge that might have broken or lost the hinge pin and was replaced by the more robust arrangement of a direct soldered attachment.

The body of the cross is very often, but not always, a cross shape. It may be simple and solid or may have an open frame-like form with various kinds of infill. Some crosses are built-up from small pieces of silver plate to construct a cross of hollow tear-shaped arms to which other embellishments are attached.

Basic cross forms often have trefoils or added serifs or terminals, of which a small diamond shape is the most frequently used.

Arm Variations

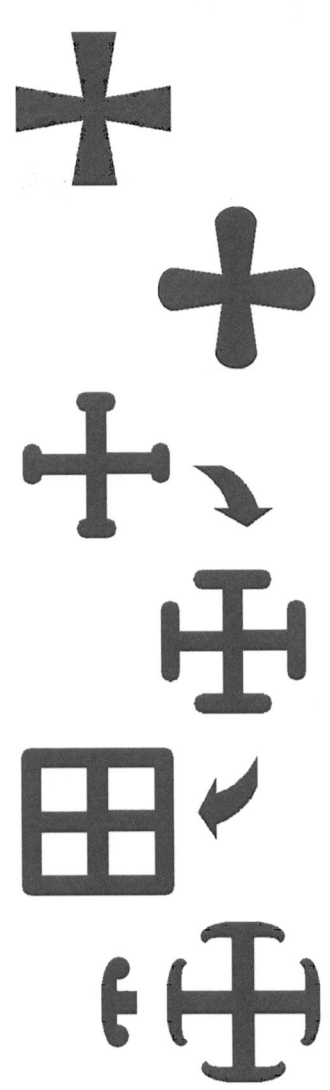

The following forms are based on the Greek (equal arms) cross although, at least for the first three variations, there are many examples with an extended leg.

The Patée cross with splayed arms

The Patée cross with splayed teardrop arms

The Greek cross with serifed arms. In variations of this form, the serifs can be extended – even to the point where they meet - to effectively form a square-enclosed cross.

Ethiopian crosses with extended serifs sometimes have pointed and inwardly curved serifs, which are representations of rams' horns. The serifs sometimes extend until they touch – and enclose the cross – and the serifs are sometimes rounded rather than pointed.

Crown Embellishments

Crosses which have the suspending ring attached to a crown element above the main body of the cross usually have a design in the middle portion of the crown and a fringe of shapes around the periphery and, in the circular forms, these edge embellishments often representing the 12 apostles.

The crown of the cross might be hinge-attached to the head of the cross or might be a directly attached extension.

There are also crosses in which the original hinge appears to have been broken and removed; and the crown has been directly silver-soldered to the cross.

The two examples of crowns on the left show signs of silver-soldering of the crown to the head of the cross (within the blue broken line) - less skilfully done in the upper example and more neatly done in the lower example.

Arm Terminals

Simple Latin or Greek-style crosses consist only of the arms of the cross and, sometimes, a ring or a crown and ring, but no terminal at the ends of the arms.

Trefoils
Trefoils are the most commonly used form of terminal at the ends of the arms of Ethiopian neck crosses. Trefoils sometimes link, or appear to link, with an endless cord infill; and the trefoil shape might have originated in cross design in its own right - e.g., as a symbol of trinity- or might have been adapted from the endless cord pattern.

Abbreviated Trefoils

Abbreviated trefoils are sometimes plain diamond-shaped terminals but more often have a pattern inscribed that consists of two lines forming a diagonal cross, with circles stamped into the spaces between the arms of the inscribed diagonal cross. This might represent the trefoil, imply the endless cord pattern, or "X" assumed to denote Χριστος (Christ).

Circles
Diamond-shaped terminals (plain trefoils) sometimes have one or more circles stamped in no specific pattern into the metal. The significance is not known, or it might simply be added as an embellishment to an otherwise plain surface.

Rectangles
Very rarely, the terminals to the arms of a cross might be unembellished rectangles.

Infills

Except for the simpler and more slender of the Ethiopian neck crosses, the width of the body and arms of the crosses are usually decorated with infill patterns either engraved into the surface or are cut through as a filigree.

Rarely, Ge'ez text might be written on the arms of a mould-cast cross, or a floral pattern might be incised.

Endless Cord Infills

The most common infill pattern is the endless cord pattern which signifies unending eternity. The pattern can be as simple as a two-loop cord in a cell of a framed cross, or an intricate filigree of multiple loops filling the entire interior of a cross or even forming the body of either a four-armed cross or a diagonal diamond-shaped cross.

Cross Infills

The second most common infill is the cross shape, orthogonal or diagonal. Cross infills may use both positive and negative cross shapes.

A positive cross is formed by the metal - as the grey cross, shown in the centre of this diagrammatic example.

A negative cross is formed by voids in the metal - as the white triangles (Patée crosses), shown in the arms of this diagrammatic example.

Circle Infills

A third pattern, usually on the terminals of the cross, but sometimes in the body of the cross, consists of small circles and dotted lines stamped into the four spaces between the arms of an inscribed diagonal cross.

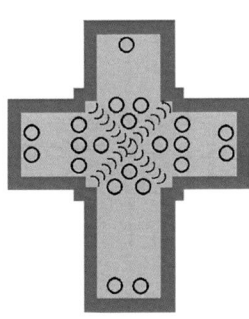

Methods, Styles and Localities

Methods of Production

There appear to be four main methods used in making neck crosses:

- Lost-wax casting
- Sand-mould or clay-mould casting
- Cutting, drilling and filing
- Cutting, assembling and soldering

In addition, embellishments might be applied or inscribed on crosses, particularly onto crosses made by either of the last two methods.

Csilla Perczel *(in the Journal* Article: *Ethiopian Crosses at the Portland Art Museum)* suggests that:

> *The lost-wax technique was traditionally used for neck crosses, which measure about 2.5–12.5 centimeters. Because they were individually cast, each one is unique. Occasionally the half mould was utilised to produce crosses with a rounded face and a flat back.*

And:

> *More recently the double mould has been used to duplicate crosses with applique decoration.*

Although Silverman and Sobania note that there is no cited evidence for this. They state that:

> *Aksum is generally held to be the historical centre for metalworking in highland Ethiopia, and to this day is regarded as one of the major centres for the production of objects in fine metals.*

And:

**A brass-alloy cross made by a casting process, possibly by lost-wax process.
The ring is clearly a soldered-on addition in different metal.**

Simoons reports that the silversmiths of northwest Ethiopia (Begemdir and Semien) maintain that their knowledge of working precious metals came from Aksum. Even today in Addis Ababa, many, if not most, of the gold and silversmiths come from either Aksum or the nearby town of Adwa. [F J Simoons, Northwest Ethiopia: Peoples and Economy, Madison 1960].

Lost-wax casting

Neck crosses, and other larger Ethiopian crosses, have been reported to be made by the lost-wax process of casting, in which the cross is first made in wax which is then enclosed in clay and the clay then dried. The clay mould is provided with a hole at the top through which molten metal can be poured and a drainage hole at the bottom through which the wax can exude when melted.

The wax might then be removed by heating and melting, after which the hole can be plugged and the molten metal can be poured into the hollow mould; alternatively, the molten metal can be poured into the mould, melting and expelling the wax. Silver melts at about 900 C, depending on the alloy, for pouring into the mould. The metal solidifies on cooling and the clay mould is broken to extract the metal cross.

Breaking the clay mould makes each cross unique although, if the initial wax model were itself made in an open mould, rather than individually cut and modelled, it would allow the same pattern to be produced repeatedly.

After removal from the clay mould, any stray metal fins are removed, and the cross is cleaned and polished to its final form. Additional patterns might then be inscribed or punched into the surface of the metal and a ring is soldered on to take the metab cord or a chain. Rings are not always of the same metal as the cross, which implies that they are attached subsequent to the casting.

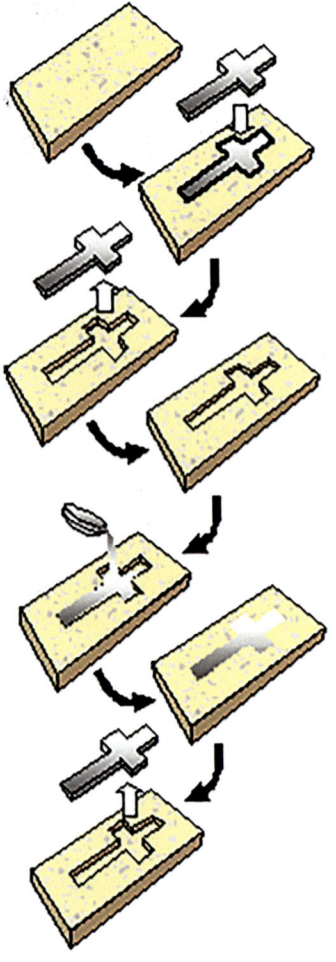

Sand-mould or clay-mould casting

Some neck crosses show, by sand-textured marks around their edges, that they were cast into a sand mould although this is more often evident in the larger hand crosses than in neck crosses.

I have not seen this process in use in Ethiopia nor found any written description of it but the process of sand moulding is much simpler than the lost-wax process, especially for flat objects patterned on one side only, and has long been used in crafts and industry in many countries and its simplicity seems to make it a more likely process than lost-wax for making small crosses.

Sand or clay moulding entails forming an impression of the cross in sand or clay (perhaps from a pattern or from an existing cross) then pouring molten metal into the open mould to form a new cross, after solidification. The sand moulding requires sand that will retain the shape of the impressed pattern and, in its simplest process, the sand is mixed with clay and contained in a small wooden box or tray. After impressing the pattern, the sand mould must thoroughly dry and harden to avoid damage that might be caused when the molten metal is poured into the mould.

If a clay mould is used and the clay is thoroughly dried or baked, it might be firm enough to not be broken when the cooled silver cross is removed from the mould and might then be re-used to produce a number of identical crosses although finer details might be eroded though subsequent castings.

The cleaning and finishing of the moulded cross is similar as for the lost-wax process and, as in the lost-wax process, if the mould is destroyed by the process, it can be recreated from the impression of the original pattern.

A video (referenced in the Weblinks list in the Appendix) made in Addis Abeba in 1969 by Watson Kintner shows a cross being made by the intricate and painstaking lost-wax process by an Ethiopian silversmith.

Cutting and soldering

There are many patterns of crosses made by silver-soldering of silver wire, silver strips or silver dots onto a plain silver cross. There are also crosses that are built up from shapes cut out of flat silver sheet, silver-soldered to make hollow forms and then have other embellishments added.

Many crosses made by this process have quite fine and intricate detail and have a finished appearance of silver jewellery.

Finishing processes

Most of the above-described methods of making metal neck crosses require finishing by filing and polishing. The casting processes might also produce fins of metal or other mould marks that have to be removed; and any casting-marks in the surface would need to be polished away.

Many crosses have surface patterns made by incising or stamping into the face of the metal. These patterns are usually made by simple tools that produce short lines or circles or dots in an arranged pattern. A very common detail is the incising of lines to represent the "cross-over" of the intersections of an endless-cord pattern. There are also instances of inscribed patterns of flowers and leaves.

Age and Wear

The age of individual crosses is difficult to assess. The styles and patterns are repeated through time - certainly through decades and perhaps across centuries - and, in the absence of any verbal or written records, the only clue to the age of an individual cross is the extent of wear or the absence of wear.

However, even this is not reliable, as crosses might be worn by people in different circumstances which might cause varied degrees of scratching and erosion and even damage to a cross, whereas a cross of similar age but worn in more benign circumstances might have much less sign of wear.

Some crosses show a greater degree of wear on one side than the other. In such instances, the less worn face usually is patterned, or more patterned than the reverse side, suggesting that it might have habitually been worn with one side shown and the other side against the body or clothes, so subject to more wear. On many crosses, the metab ring shows wear; sometimes worn more than halfway through by abrasion from a cord or chain. Some rings are worn through completely with the two parts folded together to re-form the ring.

Some crosses, especially the more delicate ones, show signs of damage or repaired breakage, particularly of the hinges which were replaced by direct soldered attachment of the crown to the cross, but this is not necessarily indicative of greater age and might simply have been due to a defective hinge.

When asked the age of a silver neck cross, the sellers in the Merkato invariably insisted that it was "very old" or "very, very old" but never stated (and clearly did not reliably know) the age as a number of years, except to guess from the visual condition of wear or damage.

The lack of signs of wear and the sharpness of the various corners in the cross at the left suggests that it might have been made relatively recently.

Styles and Localities

Various observers and travellers in Ethiopia have noted that certain styles of crosses are produced in particular localities - generally some of the principal towns of the northern provinces, especially Gondar, Axum and Lalibela.

In the small shops in the Addis Abeba Mercato, where various antiquities and artefacts were sold, the sellers often described neck crosses by locality such as Gondar, Axum, Lalibela, and Gojjam and, through the four years I was in Ethiopia, they tended to be consistent in their use of those locality designations in reference to particular styles of neck crosses.

Currently, Ethiopian neck crosses listed for sale on various internet websites are also sometimes described as being representative of various localities, although those descriptions are not always consistent or reliable.

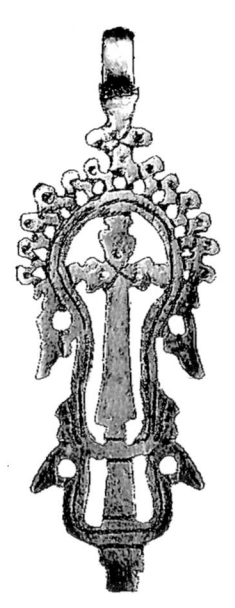

A style usually described as a Lalibela cross

It seems possible that, at least in earlier times when travel between various towns and provinces might not have been as usual as it is today, a style of cross that an artisan made in one place might become popular there and be copied and perhaps modified by others in the area and so became a style associated with that locality and thus took on its name. Also, the use of an existing cross as a pattern to impress into sand or clay moulds would facilitate the repeated production of a particular cross in a particular location. Although a style of cross might have originated in a particular location, it is probable that the various styles have subsequently been copied in many locations.

There are more than just single style-patterns of cross that are referred to by a particular locality name, but many of those style-patterns have similar characteristics even though they may not be identical or closely similar in appearance.

A style usually described as an Axum cross

Common Styles

There are several styles of neck crosses that are relatively common. Some of these styles may exist in a range of sizes - for example the plain crosses - and some may have variety in their filigree infill patterns and their surface patterning - for example, the framed and latticed crosses and particularly the medallion and hexagonal crosses.

In each case, the ring at the top of the cross might be directly attached to the cross, or the upper portion or crown of the cross might be hinge-attached. The hinged arrangement is common for larger crosses but is also found in some medium sized and small crosses.

Plain Crosses
Ethiopian plain neck crosses are more often Latin crosses than Greek crosses and they may have inscribed surface patterns or have a plain, smooth surface.

Framed Crosses
Crosses made of an outlining frame usually have a filigree infill which is most often an endless-cord diagonal pattern.

Latticed Crosses
The latticed cross is an elaboration of the framed cross with subdivided cells within the body of the cross. The interior cells of the cross usually have an infill which might be positive or negative cross patterns or simple separate endless-cord patterns within each cell. Some of these crosses are among the larger-sized neck crosses and may have the ring attached to a hinged crown or upper portion - which itself might be of an intricate design.

Medallion Crosses

In medallion style crosses the body might be based on a central cross shape (either square or diagonal), on an endless-cord pattern, on radiating arms, on star shapes or on Ethiopian shield shapes. There are often embellishments around the periphery of the body which might consist of trefoils or simplified trefoils, bird shapes, cord-like loops, or vestigial cross-arms.

Hexagonal Crosses

Neck crosses of hexagonal pattern, or Star of David pattern, might have originated with the Felasha people ("Outsiders" in Ge'ez) around Gondar in northern Ethiopia. The Felashas, who claim to be Ethiopian Jews, mostly relocated to Israel in the 1980s and 1990s although those (the Felasha Mura) who declined to renounce their Coptic Christianity and adopt Orthodox Judaism have remained in Ethiopia.

Endless Cord Crosses

The endless-cord pattern is much used as an infill in the body of Ethiopian crosses including neck crosses, and there is at least one instance of the endless-cord pattern being the entire unframed form of a neck cross with an attached metab ring.

Diamond Crosses

Ethiopian crosses also include a diamond form with an internal cross and somctimes with additional embellishments at the external corners of the diamond frame.

More elaborate diamond-shaped crosses are also common.

Octagonal Crosses

Octagonal crosses might be composed of two interwoven curved-sided squares or might be an eight-pointed star or a circle with eight small pointed loops around its perimeter. Generally, this style of cross has a cross, often a Patée cross, in the centre.

Lalibela Crosses

This is a style of cross similar to that used in the large processional crosses set on wooden shafts, in hand crosses that priests carry with them, and in neck crosses and is of a quite distinctive form and is known by name and is recognised everywhere.

It generally consists of a cross set in an elongated frame that is sometimes of a curvilinear keyhole-shape. Around the outer edge of the top half of the frame are twelve crockets which represent the twelve apostles while the lower parts of the frame are formed by the curved necks of birds whose heads and beaks face outwards.

The cross is usually surmounted by a small cross, to which the metab ring is attached, and might have a second tier of the birds' heads and curved necks below the main portion of the cross.

The degree of detail and inscribed surface patterning varies but is rarely just a plain polished finish although, in some old crosses, a considerable extent of wear might have eroded any surface patterning.

Strangely, in a three-day visit to the village of Lalibela in 1964 after a two-day trek there with mules, I did not see a single Lalibela cross.

Examples

Crosses Illustrations

The following examples of Ethiopian neck crosses are from my own collection. The illustrations are indicative of the range of neck crosses that I saw during my years in Ethiopia but there may be other styles that I never saw.

The workmanship evident in neck crosses varies considerably, perhaps due to whether the cross was made by a skilled silversmith or by an apprentice. In none of these examples is the original maker of the cross known and possibly many of the craftsmen that made these crosses, certainly the older crosses, are no longer alive; and these crosses are a small memento of the lives and work of those artisans.

All of these crosses pre-date 1973, which was the latest date that I acquired any of them, and the varying degrees of wear and, in some cases, repaired damage that they had at that time, suggest that they were then at least 20 years old and some much older. So their ages possibly range from at least as early as about 1940 to about 1950. On one cross, example 39, there are numerals that might be the date 1937 in Ge'ez calendar years, which would be 1944 in the Gregorian calendar.

The captions to the illustrations include the size and weight of each cross and an indication of the metal from which the cross is made - principally silver from Maria Theresa thalers, or of silver-copper amalgams of which the relative proportions modify the colour to some extent. In many examples the metab ring is of a different metal from the cross. The illustrations are arranged by some similarity of the crosses and, for some crosses, the locality is suggested which is characteristic of their style and from where they are purported to have come. In the illustrations, if only a single patterned side is shown, the reverse side is plain and unpatterned. The illustrations are approximately full size; and the size is measured overall including metab rings.

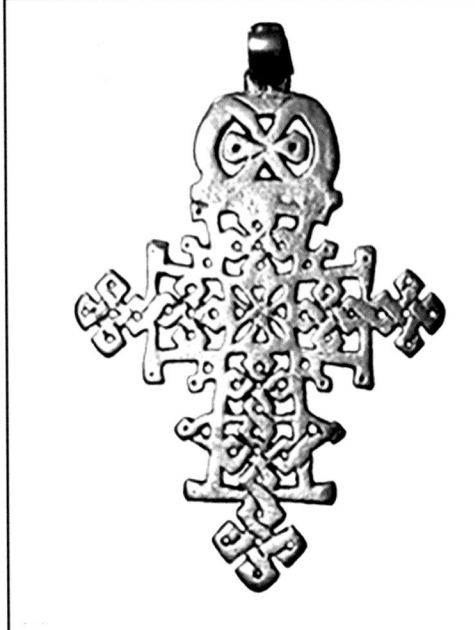

1
Style : **Axum**
Metal : **Silver alloy**
Weight : **21gm**
Size : **73 x 49mm**

The crown of this cross has been silver-soldered onto the body possibly to repair a break or perhaps to replace an original hinge that had broken

2
Style : **Axum**
Metal : **Silver alloy**
Weight : **24gm**
Size : **66 x 35mm**

An ornate framed cross with endless cord infill, serifs and trefoil terminals, and an elaborate crown.

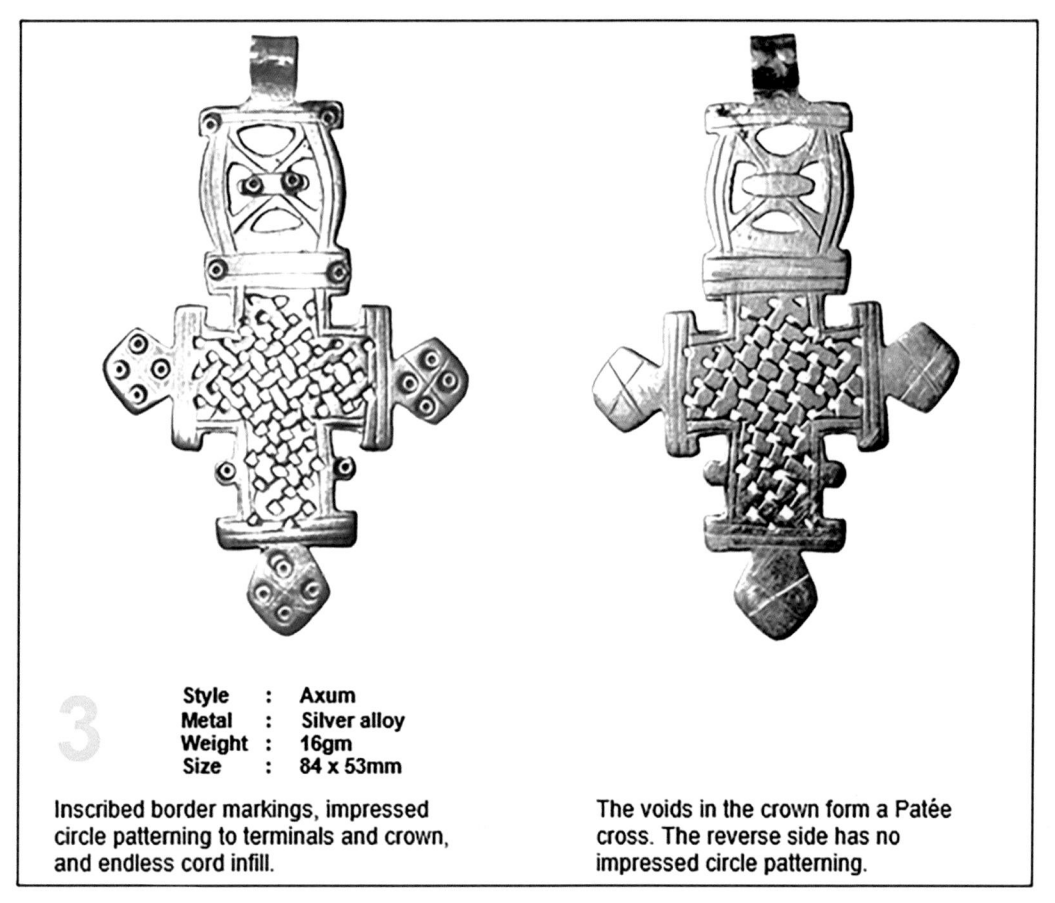

Style	:	Axum
Metal	:	Silver alloy
Weight	:	16gm
Size	:	84 x 53mm

Inscribed border markings, impressed circle patterning to terminals and crown, and endless cord infill.

The voids in the crown form a Patée cross. The reverse side has no impressed circle patterning.

4
Style : Axum
Metal : Silver alloy
Weight : 21gm
Size : 82 x 55mm

Latticed cross with infill of Patée cross voids. Inscribed diagonal markings and impressed circles cover the cross.

5
Style : Axum
Metal : Silver alloy
Weight : 18gm
Size : 78 x 49mm

Latticed cross with serifs and terminals and centre diagonal cross "X" assumed to denote Χριστος (Christ). The five cells have endless cord infills.

 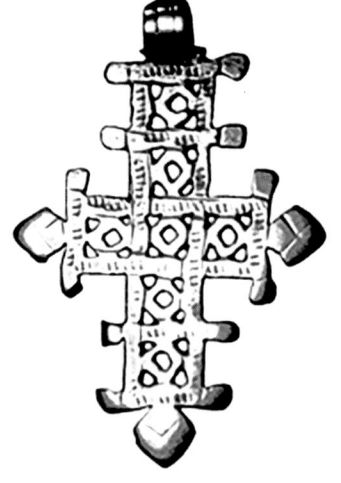

6
- **Style** : Axum
- **Metal** : Silver alloy
- **Weight** : 14gm
- **Size** : 65 x 45mm

A latticed cross with serifs and terminals, in which the lattice frame is composed of two endless cords and the cell infills imply loops of an endless cord.

The reverse side shows the same profile but with different incised patterning on the arms and no patterning on the infill elements.

7
Style : Not known
Metal : Silver alloy
Weight : 22gm
Size : 54 x 54mm

The extended serifs that meet at their extremities are representations of rams horns. The silver alloy quality of this 3mm thickness cross seems to match the Maria Theresa thaler metal.

The terminals on the reverse side have rather randomly impressed circle patterns in the trefoil terminals. The metab ring seems much newer than the cross and probably replaced a worn one.

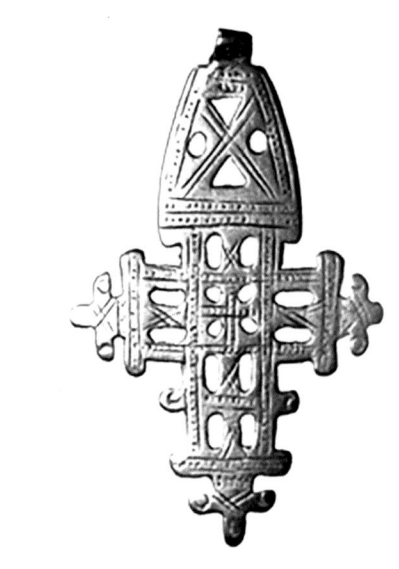

8
Style : Possibly Axum
Metal : Silver alloy
Weight : 14gm
Size : 71 x 45mm

A latticed cross with terminals and serifs and a large crown on which is inscribed an "X" assumed to denote Χριστος (Christ).

9
Style : Possibly Axum
Metal : Silver alloy
Weight : 17gm
Size : 72 x 50mm

A latticed cross with serifs and terminals, and the six cells and the crown having Patée cross infills. Large incised diagonals imply endless cords.

10
Style   : Not known
Metal   : Silver alloy
Weight : 15gm
Size   : 53 x 46mm

A cross with terminals and serifs and much incised pattering, implying endless cord.

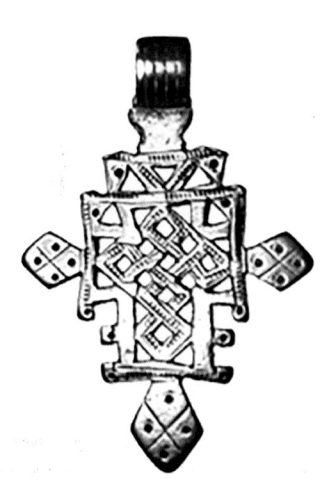

11
Style   : Not known
Metal   : Silver alloy
Weight : 12gm
Size   : 57 x 40mm

A framed cross with an infill cross composed of an endless cord. The three terminals have impressed circles in cross formation.

12

Style : Not known
Metal : Silver alloy
Weight : 12gm
Size : 54 x 40mm

A cross with incised patterns on both sides. The face shows an endless cord pattern in the arms between the terminal trefoils.

The reverse shows a simple inscribed cross pattern. The trefoils on both sides have impressed circles.

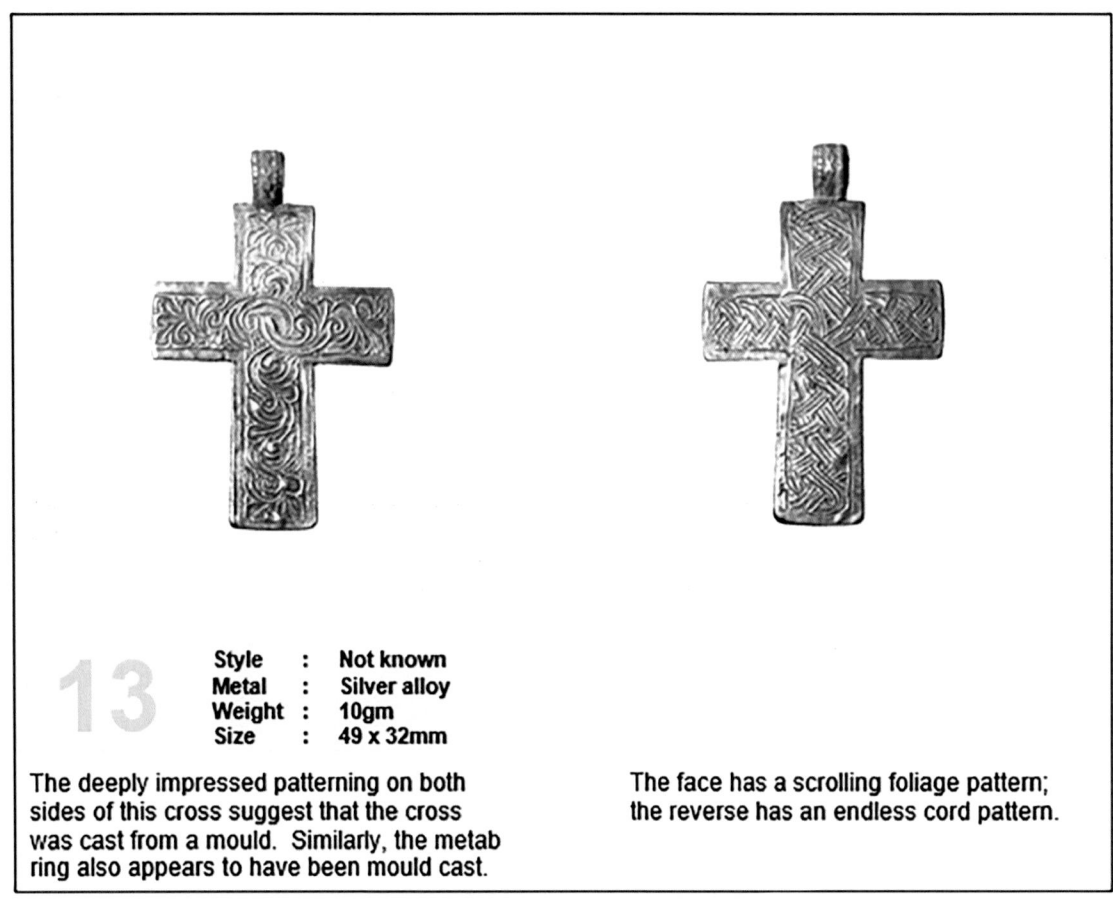

13 Style   : Not known
Metal   : Silver alloy
Weight : 10gm
Size   : 49 x 32mm

The deeply impressed patterning on both sides of this cross suggest that the cross was cast from a mould. Similarly, the metab ring also appears to have been mould cast.

The face has a scrolling foliage pattern; the reverse has an endless cord pattern.

14
Style : Not known
Metal : Silver alloy
Weight : 23gm
Size : 87 x 53mm

The hollow body and hinged triangular top is built of flat silver pieces and has cord-like silver wire around silver studs.

15
Style : Not known
Metal : Silver alloy
Weight : 15gm
Size : 80 x 50mm

A plain Latin cross with minimal pattern embellishment and a hinge-attached inverted 'U' crown.

	Style	:	Not known
16	Metal	:	Silver alloy
	Weight	:	10gm
	Size	:	59 x 35mm

A medallion or shield-like cross built from an assembly of parts on a flat silver disk; with silver wire wound around small silver beads; with a similar hinged top.

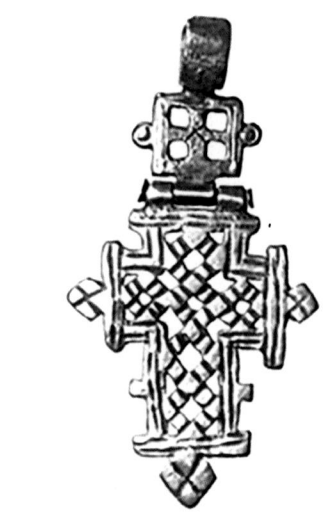

	Style	:	Possibly Axum
17	Metal	:	Silver alloy
	Weight	:	15gm
	Size	:	65 x 34mm

A framed cross with incised patterning, trefoil terminals, an endless cord infill and a hinge-attached crown in which there is a Greek cross

18
Style : Not known
Metal : Silver alloy
Weight : 8gm
Size : 43 x 23mm

A medallion style cross with thirteen perimeter segments and a centre Greek cross. The metal is a low silver-content alloy.

19
Style : Not known
Metal : Silver alloy
Weight : 8gm
Size : 45 x 24mm

A medallion style cross with nine perimeter segments. The voids in the centre form a Patée cross. The metal is a low silver-content alloy.

20

Style   : Not known
Metal   : Silver alloy
Weight : 11gm
Size   : 45 x 33mm

A circle cross with a centre Patée cross and abbreviated trefoil terminals and edge embellishments. The circle is inscribed with radial markings.

The reverse side has inscribed diagonal marking and the head suggests rams horns, Well-worn but with the inscribed patterning still visible.

21

Style : Not known
Metal : Silver alloy
Weight : 12gm
Size : 50 x 41mm

A simple cross with Patée arms around a splayed-square centre with incised border marks and impressed circles.

The reverse side includes incised triangular markings in the Patée arms and appears to also be scratched by wear.

22

Style : Not known
Metal : Silver alloy
Weight : 13gm
Size : 48 x 41mm

A Patée cross with terminals, inscribed patterns and impressed circles. The face is more elaborate than the reverse. The sharpness of the outline suggests that it had been recently made.

The metab ring patterning appears to have been mould-cast. The silver alloy of this cross gives a rather steel-like appearance to the cross.

23	Style	:	Not known
	Metal	:	Silver alloy
	Weight	:	8gm
	Size	:	45 x 41mm

A circle cross, clearly cast in a mould, with sets of triple beads forming the terminals and edge embellishments.

24	Style	:	Not known
	Metal	:	Silver alloy
	Weight	:	7gm
	Size	:	39 x 40mm

The lack of definition in this mould cast circle cross suggests that the mould had much use - with consequently eroded detail - before this cross was cast.

25

Style : Not known
Metal : Silver alloy
Weight : 13gm
Size : 44 x 45mm

An unusual square decorated plate in which the cross design is only achieved by the trefoil terminals. The crown and ring above the hinge is missing.

26

Style : Not known
Metal : Silver alloy
Weight : 7gm
Size : 43 x 38mm

A simple cross design composed of five disks with domed centres set on a flat back piece and with fine radial wire-work in each disk around each domed centre.

	Style	:	Not known
27	Metal	:	Silver alloy
	Weight	:	6gm
	Size	:	40 x 40mm

A rectilinear design of an endless cord threaded through a centre square; the inscribed marking almost entirely eroded by wear. Possibly a very old cross.

	Style	:	Not known
28	Metal	:	Silver alloy
	Weight	:	8gm
	Size	:	42 x 34mm

A framed cross with an endless cord infill. Slightly damaged and evidently well-worn.

29
Style : Not known
Metal : SilverBrass alloy
Weight : 8gm
Size : 53 x 40mm

A circle cross with a centre Patée cross and triangular terminals. Well-worn and possibly very old, with no trace of any original inscribed patterning remaining.

30
Style : Not known
Metal : Silver alloy
Weight : 12gm
Size : 53 x 38mm

A square centre and "X", assumed to denote Χριστος (Christ), reflected in chevron patterns in the Patée arms. The reverse is patterned as the face side.

	Style	:	Not known
31	Metal	:	Silver alloy
	Weight	:	9gm
	Size	:	51 x 43mm

A Greek cross form with folded silver infill patterns and silver beads to the serifs, set on a flat back piece

	Style	:	Not known
32	Metal	:	Silver alloy
	Weight	:	17gm
	Size	:	44 x 26mm

A Latin cross with rows of silver beads with very fine cord-patterning between and with small bead serifs The reverse of the cross matches the face.

33
Style   : Not known
Metal   : Silver alloy
Weight : 12gm
Size   : 47 x 42mm

An unusual design with a centre Patée cross, curving arms from serif to serif forming a larger cross, much incised patterning and cast from a mould.

34
Style   : Not known
Metal   : Silver alloy
Weight : 10gm
Size   : 45 x 37mm

A Patée cross with triangular Patée voids and triangular terminals. Well-worn and possibly very old, with no trace of any possible original inscribed patterning.

	Style	:	Not known
35	Metal	:	Silver alloy
	Weight	:	5gm
	Size	:	40 x 32mm

A circle cross with terminals forming an outer Patée-like cross. Extent of wear suggests it is very old.

	Style	:	Not known
36	Metal	:	Silver alloy
	Weight	:	8gm
	Size	:	44 x 35mm

A simplified circle cross with small triangular Patée voids and diagonal voids in the centre and very worn terminals. Extent of wear suggests it is very old.

37
Style : Not known
Metal : Silver alloy
Weight : 6gm
Size : 41 x 31mm

A simple Latin cross with an inscribed diagonal cross at the centre, impressed circles forming a cross in the arms, and fine border markings. The reverse side is similar but without the circles.

38
Style : Not known
Metal : Silver alloy
Weight : 9gm
Size : 47 x 27mm

A Latin cross with an unusual inscribed centre cross and seemingly flower-like inscribed patterns at the corners of the four arms.

39	Style	:	Not known
	Metal	:	Brass
	Weight	:	8gm
	Size	:	50 x 25mm

A Latin cross of cast brass with Ge'ez text inscriptions on both the vertical and horizontal arms on both sides of the cross; and with a much less-worn copper metab ring.

The Amharic-Ge'ez text መዘተጠምቀ ዱጸገን set vertically on the vertical arms of the face means "We are Baptised".

The Amharic-Ge'ez numerals ፲፱፻፴፯ኛ on the horizontal arm of the reverse side are "nineteen hundred thirty seven" and the letter "a", and may denote the year "1937" in Ge'ez calendar years (1944 in the Gregorian-Western calendar).

40
Style   : Not known
Metal   : Silver alloy
Weight : 8gm
Size   : 48 x 28mm

A Latin cross with an inscribed cross extending along the four arms and representing fronds or branches with leaves.

41
Style   : Not known
Metal   : Silver alloy
Weight : 6gm
Size   : 45 x 30mm

A plain and well-worn Latin cross without impressed patterns

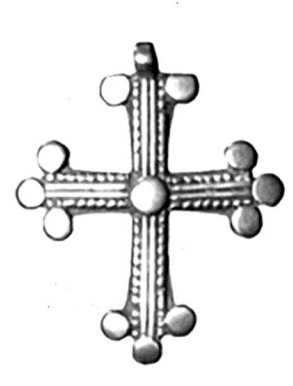

42
Style : Not known
Metal : Silver alloy
Weight : 5gm
Size : 40 x 35mm

A cast silver cross with cord-like borders to the arms and a silver stud centre with silver studs forming trefoils.

43
Style : Not known
Metal : Silver alloy
Weight : 8gm
Size : 43 x 35mm

A Greek cross with serifs and terminals, border markings to the arms and impressed circles set symmetrically.

	Style	:	Not known
44	Metal	:	Silver alloy
	Weight	:	8gm
	Size	:	45 x 44mm

A skeletal Greek cross with serifs and terminals and clearly cast from a mould. The slender arms of this cross have largely avoided damage or breakage.

	Style	:	Not known
45	Metal	:	Silver alloy
	Weight	:	5gm
	Size	:	46 x 30mm

A Latin cross with inscribed diagonal "X" (Χριστος) at the intersection of the arms, also forming a Patée cross at the centre.

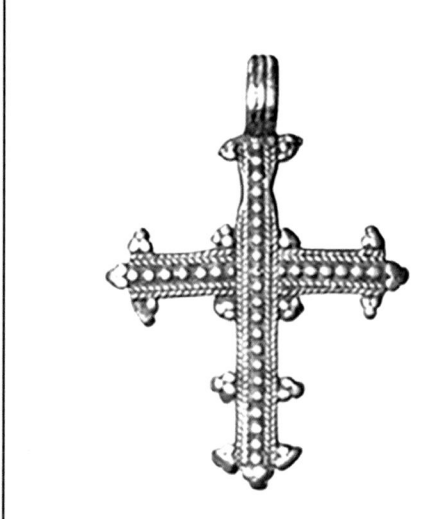

	Style	:	Not known
46	Metal	:	Silver alloy
	Weight	:	13gm
	Size	:	56 x 40mm

A cast silver Latin cross with cord-like borders beside rows of beads along the arms and small bead trefoils and serifs.

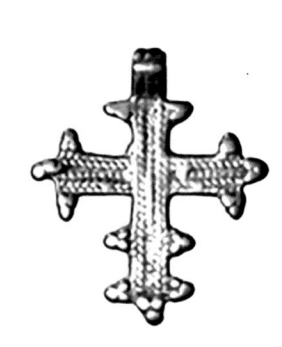

	Style	:	Not known
47	Metal	:	Silver alloy
	Weight	:	5gm
	Size	:	35 x 32mm

A cast silver cross with cord-like patterns. The lack of definition suggests that the mould had been much used and eroded before this cross was cast.

Small Crosses Illustrations

The following illustrations are of very small crosses that, judging from their small size, might have been worn by children, although the circumstances of work and play and general living conditions for many children in Ethiopia could be arduous and potentially detrimental to a small delicate cross on a cord around a child's neck.

The very small crosses available from sellers were generally fewer in number than the larger crosses. Possibly fewer were made, or possibly small crosses worn by children often became lost in the course of work or play.

As with the previous illustrations, these crosses are shown in approximately full size, measured overall including metab rings.

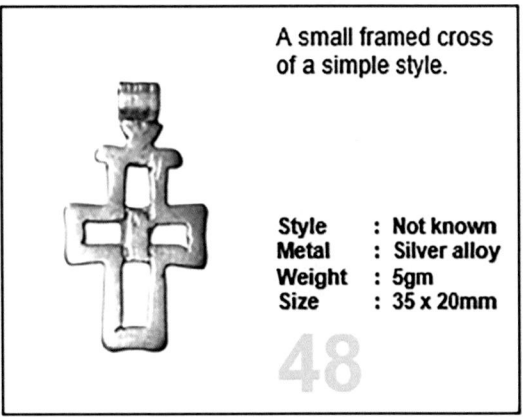

A small framed cross of a simple style.

Style : Not known
Metal : Silver alloy
Weight : 5gm
Size : 35 x 20mm

48

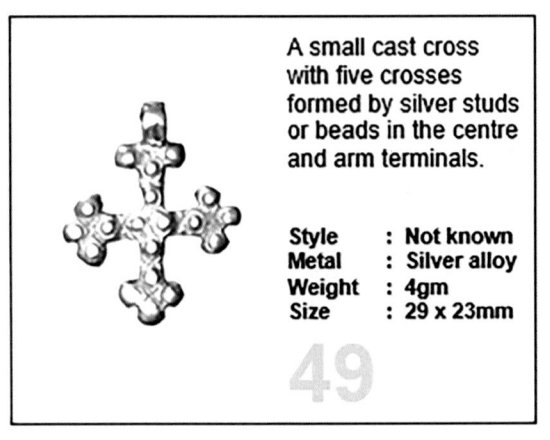

A small cast cross with five crosses formed by silver studs or beads in the centre and arm terminals.

Style : Not known
Metal : Silver alloy
Weight : 4gm
Size : 29 x 23mm

49

A small diamond-shaped cross with a circle-enclosed Patée cross in the crown.

Style : Not known
Metal : Silver alloy
Weight : 5gm
Size : 34 x 19mm

50

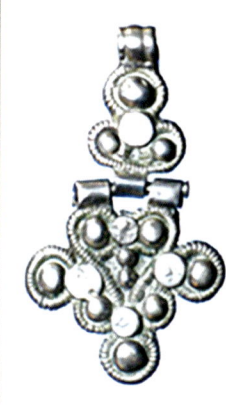

A small and unusual hinged cross of silver beads and cord surrounds, with five silver studs, perhaps added later.

Style : Not known
Metal : Silver alloy
Weight : 12gm
Size : 47 x 28mm

51

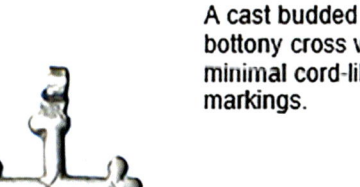

A cast budded or bottony cross with minimal cord-like markings.

Style : Not known
Metal : Silver alloy
Weight : 5gm
Size : 30 x 23mm

52

A plain Patée cross formed of round-section arms.

Style : Not known
Metal : Silver alloy
Weight : 5gm
Size : 30 x 23mm

53

A robust plain Patée cross formed of round-section arms.

Style   : Not known
Metal   : Silver alloy
Weight : 6gm
Size   : 28 x 20mm

54

A circle cross in a finger-ring-like circle with a fine cord pattern around the outside perimeter.

Style   : Not known
Metal   : Silver alloy
Weight : 5gm
Size   : 24 x 18mm

55

A very small diamond-shaped cross with inscribed cross-over markings making an endless cord.

Style   : Not known
Metal   : Silver alloy
Weight : 5gm
Size   : 23 x 16mm

56

A very small cast cross consisting of five silver studs with serifs and terminals.

Style   : Not known
Metal   : Silver alloy
Weight : 5gm
Size   : 25 x 24mm

57

 A small well-worn Patée cross with a single impressed circle at the centre. **Style** : Not known **Metal** : Silver alloy **Weight** : 5gm **Size** : 32 x 25mm 58	A tiny cast Patée cross with a disproportionately large metab ring **Style** : Not known **Metal** : Silver alloy **Weight** : 5gm **Size** : 23 x 15mm 59
A tiny cast cross consisting of five silver studs on slender arms. **Style** : Not known **Metal** : Silver alloy **Weight** : 2gm **Size** : 28 x 17mm 60	 A tiny delicate Patée cross with a hinge-attached diamond shape crown. **Style** : Not known **Metal** : Silver alloy **Weight** : 1gm **Size** : 24 x 11mm 61

Bibliography

Abbink, Jon. (2015) *The Cross in Ethiopian Christianity*. The Routledge Companion to Christianity in Africa; 7, pp 122 – 140.

Buxton, David. (1949). *Travels in Ethiopia*. London Benn.

Chojnacki, Stanisław & **Gossage**, Caroline. *Ethiopian Crosses: a Cultural History and Chronology*. Skira, Milan, 2006; & Thames & Hudson, 2010.

Di Salvo; Mario. (2006). Crosses of *Ethiopia: The Sign of Faith: Evolution and Form,* Skira, Milan.

Evangelatou, Maria (2013). *The symbolic language of Ethiopian crosses:* University of California Santa Cruz

Fisher, Angela. (1990). *Africa Adorned*. Harry N Abrams Inc, New York.

Fisher, Angela. (1990). *African Ark: People and Ancient Cultures of Ethiopia and the Horn of Africa*. Harry N Abrams Inc, New York.

Hecht, Elisabeth-Dorothea. (1986) *The Hand-cross Collection of the Institute of Ethiopian Studies: a Project Report*. Proceedings of the First International Conference on the History of Ethiopian Art. pp 115 – 120.

Huyn, Ludwig, and **Kalmer**, Josef, (1935) *Abessinien, Afrikas Unruhe-Herd*, Verlag "Das Bergland-Buch", Berlin.

Jones, Lynn. *Variations on a Theme: Hand and Processional Crosses*. Peregrinations: Journal of Medieval Art and Architecture 8, 1 (2022): 67 – 111.

Korabiewicz, Waclaw & **Turski**, S. (1973). *The Ethiopian cross*. Addis Ababa, Holy Trinity Cathedral.

Mathiesen, Sarah. (2022): *Effective Objects: Ethiopian Pectorals and the Body*. Peregrinations: Journal of Medieval Art and Architecture 8, 1 112 – 149.

Milkias, Paulos. (2011), *Africa in Focus: Ethiopia*. ABC-CLIO; California.

Moore, Eine. (1971). *Ethiopian Processional Crosses*. The Institute of Ethiopian Studies, Addis Ababa.

Pankhurst, Richard. (1997). *Ethiopian Crosses, and Their History: Processional, Hand and Neck Crosses*. Addis Tribune.

Perczel, Csilla Fabo. (1981). *Ethiopian crosses at the Portland Art Museum*. African Arts, Vol.14, No.3.

Perczel, Csilla Fabo. (1983). *Art and Liturgy: Abyssinian Processional Crosses*. Publication: Northeast African studies. 5 (1), pp 19 – 28.

Petrides, Stephanos Pierre. (1969). *The Wonderful World of Ethiopian Crosses*. Ethiopian Mirror.

Rey, Charles Fernand, (1927), [*List of Ethiopian Kings*, H.I.H. Tafari Makonnen, 1922], *In the country of the Blue Nile*, Duckworth, London.

Saul, Hans Günter. (2013). *Äthiopische Kreuze*. (Publisher not known)

Silverman, Raymond and **Sobania**, Neal. (2004). *Mining a Mother Lode: Early European Travel Literature and the History of Precious Metalworking in Highland Ethiopia*. Journal Article, History in Africa, Vol. 31 pp. 335 – 355.

Skrobucha, Heinz. (1983). *Athiopische Kreuze: Funktionen, Brauchtum, Formen*. Greven Verlagsgesellschaft Eggenkamp. Germany. OCLC 25954015.

Tadesse, Bantaleem. (2002) *The Ma'etet (Neck Band) and Cross*. Sixth International Conference on the History of Ethiopian Art: Addis Ababa, pp 371-387.

Ya Ityopyā Masqaloč: The Ethiopian Crosses. Tensae Publications House, Addis Ababa 1997.

Web-Links

Fogg, Sam. (2009). *Ethiopian Art 12th–18th Century*. Catalogue
https://www.mullenbooks.com/pages/books/152788/sam-fogg/ethiopian-art-12th-18th-century

Hamill Gallery of Tribal Art, Boston, Massachusetts
www.hamillgallery.com/ETHIOPIAN/EthiopianCrosses/CopticCrosses.html

Harding, Paul (editor) and **Boynton,** Sarah (research)
www.seiyaku.com/customs/crosses/ethiopian.html

Jones, Lynn. https://digital.kenyon.edu/perejournal/vol8/iss1/8

O'Sullivan, Katie, *Ethiopian Coptic Cross Symbology*
www.katieojewelry.com

Society for the Conservation of the Ethiopian Cultural Heritage (SCECH)
www.conservationinethiopia.org/?page_id=2

University of Pennsylvania Museum of Archaeology and Anthropology: Kintner, Watson. Film ID: F16-0377, 3m 45s—17m 09s Cat. Reel 377 1969: Reel 34: Ethiopia. April 30. Addis Ababa.
https://www.penn.museum/collections/videos/video/477

Waddington, Rod, *Orthodox Ethiopia*
www.flickr.com/groups/824735@N21/pool/rod_waddington

W. Hagos, Tecola. (2002). *The Lalibela Ethiopian Cross*.
www.tecolahagos.com/faith.htm

Wikimedia Commons: File: *Ezana.jpg*
https://commons.wikimedia.org/w/index.php?curid=3709628">Link

Wikipedia: *Christian Cross Variants*
https://en.wikipedia.org/wiki/Christian_cross_variants

Collections

A short list of Museums that have collections of Ethiopian crosses.

Museum collections generally have the more elaborate processional crosses and hand crosses, but fewer neck crosses.

The Bowers Museum, Santa Ana, California

The British Museum, London

The Coptic Museum of Canada. Toronto, Ontario

The Dallas Museum of Art, Dallas, Texas

The Metropolitan Museum of Art, New York

The Museum of Natural and Cultural History Eugene, Oregon
Bowerman Hall Collection

The Néprajzi Museum of Ethnography Budapest, Hungary

The Brooklyn Museum, Brooklyn, New York

The Virginia Museum of Fine Arts, Richmond, Virginia

The Walters Art Museum, Baltimore, Maryland

The National Museum in Warsaw (Muzeum Narodowe w Warszawie)
Wacław Korabiewicz's Collection